FAMOUS IMMIGRANT
ENTREPRENEURS

DISCARD

MAKING A~~ ~~
IMMIGRANT ~~SUCCESS STORIES~~

FAMOUS IMMIGRANT
ENTREPRENEURS

Barbara Krasner

Enslow Publishing

101 W. 23rd Street
Suite 240
New York, NY 10011
USA

enslow.com

Published in 2018 by Enslow Publishing, LLC.
101 W. 23rd Street, Suite 240, New York, NY 10011

Library of Congress Cataloging-in-Publication Data

Names: Krasner, Barbara, author.
Title: Famous immigrant entrepreneurs / Barbara Krasner.
Description: New York : Enslow Publishing, [2018] | Series: Making America
  great: immigrant success stories | Audience: Grades 7–12. | Includes
  bibliographical references and index.
Identifiers: LCCN 2017015424 | ISBN 9780766092419 (library bound) | ISBN 9780766095878
  (paperback)
Subjects: LCSH: Businesspeople—United States—Biography—Juvenile
  literature. | Immigrants—United States—Biography—Juvenile literature.
Classification: LCC HC102.5.A2 K72 2017 | DDC 338.092/69120973—dc23
LC record available at https://lccn.loc.gov/2017015424

Printed in the United States of America

Photo credits: Cover, p. 3 Mike Pont/WireImage/Getty Images; pp. 6–7 Topical Press Agency /Hulton Archive/Getty Images; pp. 9, 18 Fotosearch/Archive Photos/Getty Images; pp. 10–11 Leemage /Corbis Historical/Getty Images; pp. 14–15 Hulton Archive/Archive Photos/Getty Images; p. 21 George Rinhart/Corbis Historical/Getty Images; pp. 22–23, 24–25, 44, 46–47 Bettmann/Getty Images; p. 28 Stock Montage/Archive Photos/Getty Images; p. 32 Stefano Bianchetti/Corbis Historical /Getty Images; pp. 34–35 imageBROKER/Alamy Stock Photo; pp. 36–37 Archive Photos /Getty Images; p. 41 National Archive/Newsmakers/Hulton Archive/Getty Images; p. 45 Peter Charlesworth/LightRocket/Getty Images; p. 49 Steve Hansen/The LIFE Images Collection /Getty Images; p. 55 Anne Knudsen/Hulton Archive/Getty Images; p. 57 Keystone-France/ Gamma-Keystone/Getty Images; p. 59 Rae Russel/Archive Photos/Getty Images; p. 61 Christopher J. Morris/Corbis Historical/Getty Images; p. 65 Yvonne Hemsey/Hulton Archive /Getty Images; p. 66 RDA/Hulton Archive/Getty Images; p. 67 Yamaguchi Haruyoshi/Corbis Entertainment/Getty Images; pp. 68–69 NetPhotos/Alamy Stock Photo; p. 75 Andy Freeberg /Bloomberg/Getty Images; pp. 78–79 Katherine Frey/The Washington Post/Getty Images; p. 83 Eco Images/Universal Images Group/Getty Images; pp. 86–87 Peter Foley/Bloomberg /Getty Images; pp. 88–89 David Jay Zimmerman/Corbis Documentary/Getty Images; pp. 90–91 Jules Annan/Barcroft Media/Getty Images; p. 93 Albin Lohr-Jones/Bloomberg /Getty Images; cover and interior pages Saicle/Shutterstock.com (flag).

Contents

Introduction

America has been a land of immigrants for hundreds of years. People came from other countries seeking a chance to have a better life. For some, a new life in America meant adventure or an opportunity to leave behind the strict rules of their homelands. For others, immigration meant leaving behind poverty and joblessness. And for religious minorities or people in war zones, immigration meant the possibility of religious freedom or peace. Traditionally, the melting pot of America has attracted talented individuals from all over the world.

By the nineteenth century, immigrants had established themselves in many types of businesses, including retail, manufacturing, and finance. The twentieth century brought opportunities for immigrants to distinguish themselves in all of these fields, as well as technology.

People who start their own businesses are called entrepreneurs. And to be successful, entrepreneurs must bring a team of people together to realize their vision. The immigrant entrepreneurs covered in this book are no different. By creating jobs, these immigrants have given the US economy a boost. In fact, immigrants (or their children) founded more than 40 percent of Fortune 500 companies.[1] Foreign-born entrepreneurs launched well-known American companies such as AT&T, Colgate, Pfizer Pharmaceutics, Anheuser-Busch, Goldman Sachs, and Procter & Gamble. Newer companies, many of them focused on technology, also owe their existence to the visions of their founders. These include Google, eBay, and Yahoo!

Workers in countries outside the United States, like these hat workers in Manchester, England, often brought highly desirable skills with them that benefited American industry when they moved to the United States.

The percentage of immigrant entrepreneurs is greater than the percentage of foreign-born people in the United States, according to census data.[2] So, immigrants not only use their business savvy to create opportunities for themselves but also for America as a whole. These business innovators have a lot in common. They know how to connect with important people in their industries and add them to their networks. They have big ideas and a vision. Many faced difficulties early in life. The troubles of the past motivate them to give back to others through philanthropy. They give their time and money to thank individuals and organizations that helped them along the way.

Each immigrant entrepreneur this book covers has ties to well-known companies. German immigrant Levi Strauss founded the blue jeans company bearing his name. Scottish immigrant Andrew Carnegie founded Bethlehem Steel and gave away his millions to found public libraries and organizations. Scottish immigrant Alexander Graham Bell gave us the telephone and cofounded the Bell Company, which later became AT&T. Chinese immigrant An Wang started his Wang Laboratories in the early days of computing. Hungarian immigrant Andy Grove cofounded Intel, makers of the Pentium and other computer chips. Greek immigrant Arianna Huffington founded media company the Huffington Post. Indian immigrant Vinod Khosla started Sun Microsystems and, as a venture capitalist, helps fund and mentor other entrepreneurs. Finally, Russian immigrant Sergey Brin is cofounder of Google.

Without immigrant innovation and talent, it is fair to say America would not have the reputation it has for being the land of opportunity. These entrepreneurs prove it.

CHAPTER 1

LEVI STRAUSS MAKES AMERICAN DENIM PANTS FAMOUS

Levi Strauss was born Loeb Strauss in Bavaria, Germany, in 1829. His father, Hirsch, was a cattle trader, and his mother, Rebecca, was the daughter of a cattle trader. Loeb was their last child and their only son; the couple also had a daughter. Hirsch, however, had five children before his second marriage to the much younger Rebecca.

Life wasn't easy for this Jewish family in their village of Buttenheim. Germany introduced new laws against Jews in the early 1800s. According to these laws, Jews couldn't own land and work certain jobs. But Hirsch ignored the law and kept working as a trader. His son Jacob, however, decided to leave home for England and make a new life for himself there. His daughter Roesla

Levi Strauss, shown here about 1850, managed to work for his family's business while also branching out on his own.

Before steamships made travel more efficient, it took immigrants like Levi Strauss weeks or months to journey to the United States in ships like the ones pictured in Boston Harbor around 1850.

decided on America and left in 1837. Jonathan followed in 1840 and Lippman in 1841.

WHEN ONE DOOR CLOSES, ANOTHER OPENS

After Hirsch died in 1846 at the age of fifty-six, Rebecca married his brother. But he died just a few weeks later. Rebecca felt it would be best for the rest of her family—Levi and two older sisters—to join Jonathan (now Jonas) and Lippman (now Louis) in New York. Leaving the country took courage and patience. The government had to grant permission for the Strausses to leave. It took nearly a year of paperwork and finding a ship traveling to New York from the German port of Bremen.

The voyage may have taken more than two months. Once in New York City in 1848, Loeb and his family settled into Little Germany, a neighborhood on the Lower East Side. During the 1840s, thousands of Germans had immigrated and by living in one area, they could speak their native language and keep practicing their customs.

Jonas and Louis had started a wholesale dry goods business, living above the store. Dry goods include thread, cloth, and personal care items. By 1850, Jonas and Louis had a servant, so the business must have been doing well. Levi became one of the store's traveling

FROM PEDDLER TO TYCOON

Strauss's brothers began as street peddlers and built up their dry goods business from there. America welcomed street peddlers in the nineteenth century. Peddling for many turned into respected and profitable businesses. Adam Gimbel stands out as a success among German-Jewish immigrants. Gimbel came from Germany's Rheinland-Pfalz region at age eighteen with no money. He peddled goods from farm to farm in Indiana. Peddling allowed immigrants to earn money and get to know their American customers better.

Gimbel moved to Milwaukee, Wisconsin, and took advantage of that city's population and economic boom. He took over a Philadelphia department store and then opened a store in New York City, competing with the famous Macy's department store. Gimbel's operated from 1887 to 1987 and made Adam Gimbel a rich man.

Levi Strauss and his brothers followed a similar model. They worked as street peddlers, opened one store, and then multiple stores in different cities. But Levi took the business even farther by getting a patent, a government-issued license that prevents copycats from selling and profiting from someone else's invention.

salesmen and even applied for US citizenship. But he felt restless; he wanted to be on the move. His sister Fanny married another Jewish immigrant peddler, David Stern, and moved with him to St. Louis. Levi decided to strike out on his own, too, using his ties to the family business to travel. In Kentucky, he distributed merchandise from his brothers' store.

GOLD!

Despite their physical distance from each other, the Strausses stayed in contact. When the California Gold Rush struck, they chose young, single Levi to set up shop on the West Coast. They wanted to take advantage of the sales opportunity. Miners would need clothes, but most could not afford to have them tailored (made with their exact measurements). They could, however, pay for shirts, pants, and vests that were ready to wear.

In the 1900s, traveling to California from the East Coast wasn't easy. Heading West meant taking one of two sea routes: Cape Horn in South America or Panama in Central America. Either way, the journey would be hard and dangerous. Still, the Strausses loaded dry goods from their store on the *Winged Racer*, a boat that would take the first route. Newly a US citizen, Levi boarded a US mail steamship that would take him to Panama. He wanted to reach San Francisco, the center of the gold rush, before the *Winged Racer*. Although it took nearly two months of travel and traveling by train, boat, and mule in Panama, Levi boarded another ship there and headed first to Mexico and then along the California coast. The twenty-four-year-old did indeed arrive before his merchandise in March 1853 and awaited the arrival of two more shiploads. His mission was to set up a store on the waterfront. Using connections to merchants his family would have had with other San Francisco Jews, Levi would get help and not be alone. He introduced himself to local retailers but knew he would

The Gold Rush of 1849 brought miners and immigrants to the West. Chinese immigrants, like the ones shown here in 1855, came to the United States in droves to strike it rich. Levi Strauss sold such miners sturdy clothes.

eventually have to get to the miners. He traveled out to Sacramento and other communities, racking up a number of customers along the way. Back in San Francisco, he had business letterhead printed and prepared for the fall season.

Strauss lived and worked in a rough-and-tumble city that offered plenty of pleasurable distractions and crime. In 1853, San Francisco had 399 saloons, 28 breweries, and 1,200 reported murders. More than one thousand ships lay abandoned in the harbor, their crews sidetracked by the gold craze. More than seven thousand new arrivals to the city simply vanished, never to be seen again.[1]

But Strauss kept his focus and his efforts paid off—handsomely.

THE FAMILY BUSINESS THRIVES IN CALIFORNIA

Over the next couple of years, Levi Strauss fell into a routine. Ships arrived from New York, and he continued to find new customers for the new merchandise. By 1855, Strauss was sending gold back home, both to give to his brothers and to purchase more dry goods. Although a financial panic broke out in San Francisco, Strauss was

"THE SECRET OF THEM PENTS IS THE RIVETS"[2]

In his 1872 letter, Davis made it clear that the pants with the riveted pockets were in high demand. He couldn't make them fast enough. But he knew his jealous neighbors wanted to compete against him. He knew that he would have to protect his invention with a patent. He said the patent would cost sixty-eight dollars and in exchange for Strauss giving him that money, Davis would give him a 50 percent right to sell the patented clothing. Davis noted, though, that Strauss could sell the pants in certain states and territories, and Davis would retain the rights for the rest of the country. Davis suggested a retail price of three dollars per pair or thirty dollars per dozen.

For Strauss, Davis's proposal meant real profits. The pants his company manufactured only sold for ten dollars a dozen. Levi accepted the proposal. He applied for the patent "to prevent the seam from starting or giving away from the frequent strain or pressure,"[3] but the US Patent Office rejected the application. It stated there were too many other similar patents for clothing with rivets. Strauss and Davis kept at it and after three revisions and months of haggling, their application finally met with approval on May 20, 1873—the day blue jeans were born.

able to maintain gold payments worth millions in today's currency. Soon Strauss welcomed the arrival of his sister Fanny and her family to San Francisco. It is likely that his mother came to join her two children, too. Strauss was now prepared to benefit both professionally and personally. He brought his brother-in-law into the business.

THE BIRTH OF LEVI STRAUSS & CO.

By 1863, the company changed to Levi Strauss & Company to reflect the addition of David Stern to the firm. But another addition would brand the company forever.

A Jewish immigrant tailor named Jacob Davis was making and selling duck twill and blue denim pants with riveted pockets. He bought the fabric from Levi Strauss, usually on credit. Despite two patents, he could barely make a living. He wrote to Levi on July 2, 1872, offering his invention. In response, Strauss offered Davis a partnership.

Davis, however, lacked the salesmanship and grasp of the English language that Strauss had, and he soon sold his half of the business to him. By the end of their first year, they made more than $40,000 from the pants Strauss called "waist overalls."[4] More than twenty thousand men[5] were wearing the pants with the recognizable orange thread Davis used to match the rivets. Strauss opened a factory in San Francisco to keep up with demand.

STEPPING BACK FROM BUSINESS DEMANDS

At home, Strauss's sister gave him a comfortable and loving place to live. At the office, he liked to spend time catching up with his workers and refused to be called Mr. Strauss. He wanted to be called Levi. Business soared and sales representatives were making good in

In this photograph, two gold miners sport their Levis blue jeans outside the Last Chance Mine in Northern California's "Gold Country" around 1882. Last Chance got its name when a starving miner used his last bullet to shoot a deer for food.

Mexico and across the Pacific in Hawaii, Tahiti, and New Zealand. In 1880, Levi Strauss & Co. had 250 workers and sales of $2.4 million. Strauss took pride in knowing he was clothing the workingman— the farmer, mechanic, miner, cowboy, and laborer. But as he aged, he let his nephews take charge of the business. In 1890, the patent ran out. That meant competitors were now free to copy the jeans. A multimillionaire, Strauss turned to philanthropic activities. He was a trustee of the Pacific Hebrew Orphan Asylum and the Eureka Benevolent Society. He also established twenty-eight scholarships at the University of California.[6]

THE LEGACY OF LEVI STRAUSS

Strauss died in 1902 at the age of seventy-three. Since he did not marry or have children, his will stated that his money be given to his nephews and donated to charities, such as his own Levi Strauss Foundation. The name of an immigrant entrepreneur lives on, printed on red tabs sewn onto the back pockets of his denim pants. They have been woven into the fabric of American life, from Western wear to the all-American staple, especially for young people. Five generations of Strauss's family led the company through the twentieth century and into the twenty-first. Family members remain on the company's board of directors.

CHAPTER 2

ANDREW CARNEGIE BECOMES THE QUINTESSENTIAL CAPTAIN OF INDUSTRY

A ndrew Carnegie was born in Dunfermline, Scotland, in 1835. The town was known for the manufacture of fine linen. Carnegie's father, Will, was a handloom weaver and helped create the Tradesman's Subscription Library. Young Andrew loved to hear men at the library discuss the books they were reading. As factories, or industrialization, spread, hand-trades became less important to the economy. Andrew had to drop out of school at age eleven when his father lost his job.

BOOKS PROVIDE OPPORTUNITY FOR ADVANCEMENT

Financial troubles brought thirteen-year-old Andrew, his parents, and younger brother to America in 1848. They arrived in New York but settled in Allegheny, Pennsylvania, a suburb of Pittsburgh, where the family had relatives. Once again, Andrew's father took up his trade as a weaver in his own shop, but it failed and Andrew needed to earn money to help out the family.

Scottish immigrant Andrew Carnegie, in an official portrait in 1900, earned a reputation for hard-headed business and generous philanthropy that set a standard for future generations of immigrant entrepreneurs.

As a young boy, Andrew proved himself to be hardworking and ambitious. He worked in a cotton mill and as a telegram messenger boy. His fellow messengers introduced him to a man who invited him to borrow books from his personal library. The library became Carnegie's key to opening the world. Denied a formal education by poverty, he could educate himself through books. Andrew placed great importance on books. He read in every available moment and devoured the pages. He relied on public libraries and later said there was "no use to which money could be applied so productive...as a public library."[1]

He said that if he ever became wealthy, he would make libraries available to the poor. He taught himself telegraphy and later became a telegraph operator. While an operator, he made important contacts with people at the Pennsylvania Railroad. At age eighteen, he began working for the railroad. The railroads meant the future and progress. They represented the height of technology. Carnegie learned the railroad

Carnegie invested his money in the building of free public libraries as well as his own private library, one of sixty-six rooms, in his home at 93rd Street and Fifth Avenue in New York City.

industry and business practices in general. He absorbed everything he learned. His boss told him about the sale of ten shares of stock in the Adams Express Company. Carnegie's mother, Margaret, mortgaged the family home to give him the money to buy the shares. He saw that investments, shrewd investments, would yield additional earnings through dividends. His boss also offered him a share in the Woodruff Sleeping Car Company. Carnegie accepted the offer through a bank loan and never looked back. By age twenty-four, he was promoted to the position of superintendent for the Pennsylvania Railroad. He remained with the railroad for twelve years. During that time, he invested his earnings in other railroad ventures, oil wells, iron works, and Great Lakes steamers.

IRON AND STEEL

In 1865, he left the railroad and joined the management of the Keystone Bridge Company. This company replaced wooden railroad

Railroads in the mid-1800s provided Carnegie and others with a profitable opportunity for investment. The railroads also gave Carnegie his start in business. He learned from the people around him and from books, a lifelong practice that served him well.

bridges with iron bridges. But it was steel that attracted Carnegie's attention. He started the Carnegie Steel Corporation. He opened his first steel mill in Braddock, Pennsylvania, in 1875. Carnegie Steel became the largest steel manufacturer in the world, larger than

"THE PATRON SAINT OF LIBRARIES"[2]

In the 1800s, libraries were private establishments. Women's groups, merchants, and other business owners maintained collections of books, and patrons purchased subscriptions to the libraries. During the second half of the 1800s, a movement in America insisted that libraries be free to the public. Free public libraries helped immigrants and the poor rise up in the world, as Carnegie did. But free public libraries required money. Some communities paid for libraries by having residents pay a tax to fund them.

Carnegie's love of books and reading combined with his mission of charitable giving. He believed borrowing books should be free. He donated $55 million to fund the building of 2,509 libraries in the United States and abroad between 1886 and 1919.[3] Communities had to complete an application that required information on the size of the town, the number of books, and current circulation. They had to agree to find a location for the library and to accept Carnegie's donation.

Many Carnegie libraries still exist. Some serve different purposes now, such as museums, offices, and civic centers. Their conservation is a topic at national historic preservation conferences.

Britain's entire steel industry. Carnegie, obsessed with technology, made steel affordable. Whenever new technology became available, he replaced machines that used older technology.

Although his mills were among the most productive in the world, they came at a cost. Whistles signaling danger could be heard at any of his steel mill sites. Safety was, unfortunately, not a priority. Many accidents occurred. In 1892, a disagreement about wages between the steel company and the Amalgamated Association of Iron and Steel Workers turned into a fight at the Homestead Mill. At the time, Carnegie had a partner, Henry Clay Frick. Away in Scotland at the time, Carnegie told Frick to do whatever was necessary to restore order. So Frick closed the mill, although the union was willing to negotiate. Nearly four thousand workers were locked out as a result. Frick hired three hundred Pinkerton detectives to address the union dispute. The detectives, however, were met with stones and bullets. Nearly the whole town participated in the fight. To combat the Pinkerton rifles, workers and their families gathered all the arms they could find, including a cannon. The struggle continued for twelve hours. The Pinkertons raised the white flag of surrender four times, and each time the workers shot down the flag. The violence appalled Carnegie. The Pennsylvania governor sent in 8,500 troops to restore order. Martial law was declared. In the end, the union was crushed. Carnegie slashed five hundred jobs, lowered wages, and insisted on twelve-hour workdays.[4]

Carnegie blamed the events at Homestead Mill on Frick, with whom he'd always had a tense relationship. Carnegie proved he was the one in charge. He made that clear early on in the partnership that began in 1881 when Frick needed money to expand his coke manufacturing operations, and Carnegie needed coke. Carnegie took financial control of Frick's company, and

This color engraving from 1886 shows the Bessemer process of forging iron into steel at the Carnegie Steel Works in Pittsburgh, Pennsylvania. This process removed impurities from the iron while keeping costs down, a requirement for a successful steel business.

in turn, Frick took control of Carnegie's workers. Still, Carnegie recognized Frick's business abilities and named him chairman of Carnegie Steel in 1889. After the Homestead incident, they parted ways on bitter terms.

Carnegie sold the company in 1901 to J. P. Morgan's United States Steel Company for $480 million, $250 million of which was for personal gain.[5]

Some believed Carnegie was a greedy businessman who sacrificed his workers' needs for money. But the fact that Carnegie gave so much money away to charity paints a different picture of the entrepreneur.

RETIREMENT FROM BUSINESS, ENGAGEMENT IN PHILANTHROPY

In 1868, Carnegie wrote a letter to himself that expressed his vision: to retire at age thirty-five, to live on $50,000 per year of income, and to give the rest of his money away to charity.[6] He made good on his promises to himself, although not in the timeframes he expected.

His financial plans affected his wife, too. Before the fifty-two-year-old Carnegie married thirty-year-old Louise Whitfield in 1887, Whitfield had to sign an agreement testifying that she understood what he planned to do with his money. Two years later he wrote *Gospel of Wealth*. This book explained how Carnegie believed that rich men should serve only as trustees of their money, live modestly, and use their assets to help others. He was widely praised for this view, and he proved his own beliefs with action. In 1911 he founded the Carnegie Corporation of New York. He dedicated this foundation, his last, to promote education and peace. Carnegie served as its first president.

THE CARNEGIE LEGACY

Local or international organizations bearing the Carnegie name, either wholly or in part, received funding from Andrew Carnegie. For example, in 1895, he established the Carnegie Museums of Pittsburgh with a $20 million endowment. It includes an art gallery, museum of natural history, music hall, and library.

In 1900, he gave $2 million to some Pittsburgh technical schools. These schools combined to form the Carnegie Institute of Technology. In 1967, the Institute merged with the Mellon Institute to become Carnegie Mellon University, a prestigious school that attracts some of the best young scientists, artists, writers, and entrepreneurs.

Carnegie set his sights on Washington, DC, in 1902. With $22 million, he founded the Carnegie Institution of Washington, dedicated to scientific discovery. There, scientists worked on research that resulted in radar and biotechnologies. It is now known as the Carnegie Institution for Science.

In 1903, he founded the Carnegie Foundation with $1.5 million to build a courthouse and library for the Permanent Court of Arbitration in the Netherlands' capital city, The Hague. The building became known as the Peace Palace. The following year, he founded the Carnegie Hero Fund Commission to recognize people who take action to rescue their fellow man. The commission took its inspiration from a Pennsylvania coalmine disaster that claimed the lives of workers who tried to help others. Hero funds are now used in the United States, the United Kingdom, and throughout Europe.

Although extremely successful in America, Carnegie never forgot his roots. In 1903, he started the Carnegie Dunfermline Trust to help the twenty-six thousand people in his hometown. The $4 million trust has touched nearly every part of life in the community for adults and youth.[8]

A MISSION FOR WORLD PEACE

Toward the end of his life, Carnegie realized he still had not given away all his money. A pacifist—a person who doesn't believe in war—he hoped for world peace. He believed that any future conflicts could be prevented through negotiation. He gave $10 million to establish the Carnegie Endowment for International Peace in 1910. He worked tirelessly in the name of peace until World War I broke out. He died in 1919, two months after the Treaty of Versailles was signed, disappointed that his efforts had failed. But he had given away $350 million to deserving causes.[7]

Immigrant Andrew Carnegie started as a teen who chose to educate himself and work up the business ladder. The path was not always easy. He is considered one of America's wealthiest businessmen with nearly three times the assets of billionaires Bill Gates or Warren Buffett.[9]

CHAPTER 3

ALEXANDER GRAHAM BELL GETS WIRED

Alexander Graham Bell was born in Edinburgh, Scotland, in 1847. Both his grandfather and his father, Melville, were experts on how the voice worked, and they taught speech and elocution (how to speak properly, especially in public). Bell did not want to follow in his father's footsteps but could not escape his destiny.

THE EARLY YEARS

Alexander's mother, Eliza, was nearly deaf but became a pianist. Her accomplishment inspired young Alexander to think and act big. Alexander demonstrated great musical ability. He could play the piano by ear and dreamed of becoming a great musician. His natural talent for hearing even the slightest change in sound would serve him well later. He

In this colorized photograph from 1892, Alexander Graham Bell, surrounded by 150 observers at AT&T in New York, leads a demonstration of a long-distance telephone call.

A LIFELONG PASSION FOR DISCOVERY

Alexander had much in common with his grandfather, after whom he was named. Like him, Alexander loved to learn. He especially enjoyed science and art. He longed to know how the world around him worked and went to London to live with his grandfather at age fourteen. There, his grandfather taught him elocution, Shakespeare, how to dress, and how to treat speech defects.

With his father the following year, he went to visit Sir Charles Wheatstone, rumored to have a machine that could pronounce words. Alexander observed the machine, and although he thought it pretty basic, it made a great impression on him.

When presented with an opportunity to solve a problem through technology, he eagerly accepted. Although he earned a reputation of flying from one idea to another, his dedication to solving problems led to important discoveries.

also continued to play piano the rest of his life, although dreams of becoming a musician faded over time.

Eliza home-schooled him. He did not prove to be a great student, but he had a natural ability to solve problems. For example, at eleven years old, a friend's father challenged Alexander to come up with a way to remove husks from wheat grain. After studying the situation, he built a device with paddles and brushes that quickly removed the husk from the grain. This was his first real invention, and he knew it was important. He later said that from that moment on he knew he could be useful to others and was thankful that his friend's

Like the human vocal system, the piano is a complex system that can manipulate musical sounds. Bell's passion for music helped with his voice work. He likely played a piano like the nineteenth-century German instrument shown here.

father gave him the opportunity to invent.

Then Melville invited him and one of his brothers to develop a device that could top Wheatstone's and produce human speech more accurately. The boys divided up the tasks. Using a human skull and rubber, wood, wire, and cotton, they made a machine they controlled with a keyboard. They tested it on the stairway of a building in a nearby square and "made it yell."[1] Passersby thought they heard a baby crying. The experiment taught Bell about the value of hard work and patience. It also taught him about vocal chords.

Alexander became very familiar with his father's work in Visible Speech, a system of symbols that recreated the sounds of tongue and lips. This system, Melville concluded, could be useful in working with the deaf. Sympathetic to the cause because of his mother's hearing impairment, young Bell joined his father in his work with the deaf and eventually took over his father's London operations. He also became a teacher of English and received praise from school masters for keeping students engaged.

The capital city of Edinburgh in Scotland dates back to the Middle Ages. In Bell's time, the city suffered from overcrowding, over-industrialization, lack of sanitation, and poverty. While it offered great opportunity for learning, living there presented many challenges.

Melville thought America would be a healthier place to live, away from the dirt and grime of Edinburgh. Bell objected at first. But then his two beloved brothers died of tuberculosis and Eliza feared for his life, too. The family moved to London and then Ontario, Canada, in 1870.

TEACHER OF THE HEARING-IMPAIRED

For a while, Bell used the new family home on ten acres (four hectares) in Brantford, Ontario, as his base. He taught the hearing-impaired at a variety of institutions throughout New England, spreading the word about his father's Visible Speech system. Boston, in particular, attracted him and he moved there in 1871. Bell viewed the city as the American center of intellectual life as well as the center of new technology. Eager to earn money to establish himself financially independent—and to attract a wife—Bell began to experiment with telegraphy, then on the cutting edge of innovation.

"MR. WATSON, COME HERE"

Bell had an idea in mind for his new invention. He wanted to develop a device to enable transmission of several telegrams at different frequencies over a single wire (harmonic telegraph). He was in a race against Thomas Alva Edison and Chicago's Elisha Gray, who had plenty of financial backing and support from the Western Union Company. By the fall of 1874, Bell's research put him ahead of Gray and closer to Edison. His loved ones feared for his health; he was obsessed with the invention. But when he tried to file a patent he learned that because he was not a US citizen, he could not file for his incomplete invention. This led him to drop the project. Edison won public praise, even though he could only transmit four messages with his device. Bell believed he could deliver eight.

Back in Brantford, Bell gathered all he knew about teaching the deaf and telegraphy. There, he developed the basic design of the telephone, transmitting voice over the wires. He invited backing from the parents of his students, such as Boston attorney Gardiner Greene Hubbard. Hubbard's daughter, Mabel, had lost her hearing after catching scarlet fever. Hubbard became a partner, as did Thomas Saunders, the father of another student, George. Hubbard checked for existing patents and found none. But Bell knew Gray was closing in on the same telephone idea. It would be a race to the finish.

In 1875, Thomas Watson worked as Bell's assistant. Together, they continued the work on multiple telegraphy, which Hubbard believed would bring great profits. But in the midst of this work, Bell stumbled upon a discovery that excited him even more: transmitting sound vibrations over wire. He continued work on the telephone, despite the objections of his family, Hubbard, and Saunders. And once engaged to Mabel, he had even more reason to forge ahead. Again, he met with patent challenges from Gray and Edison. Finally, on March 3, 1876, he won the patent for the telephone. A week later, Bell tested

"MY GOD, IT TALKS!"

To promote the telephone, Bell conducted a demonstration at the 1876 Centennial Exhibition in Philadelphia. Emperor Dom Pedro of Brazil, who had visited Bell at the Boston School for the Deaf, attended the event. Visible Speech fascinated him. Dom Pedro took part in the demonstration, yelling out, "My God, it talks!" Then, he dropped the "tele-phone."[3]

Elisha Gray also attended the demonstration. He heard, "Aye, there's the rub,"[4] a quote from Shakespeare's play "Hamlet." He admitted to the scientists in attendance that it was the first time he heard words from an electric telephone. Later that day, Bell and Gray agreed to work together on multiple telegraphy.

his new device. On the telephone, Watson heard, "Mr. Watson, come here. I want you." And Bell heard, "Mr. Bell, do you understand what I say?"[2] In a letter to his father, Bell revealed he thought the telephone had solved a great problem. It would someday allow friends to have a conversation without leaving home.

THE BELL TELEPHONE COMPANY

Bell's successful invention led to the opening of the Bell Telephone Company in 1877. He served as the company's technical adviser. Bell was clearly not following in his father's footsteps now, but his path was by no means clear. Over the next twenty years, competitors brought 550 lawsuits again him, challenging his patent.[5] None of these actions succeeded, and Bell continued to create. He added Thomas Edison's microphone to the telephone so shouting was no longer necessary.

Bell knew that he was no real businessman. He was more interested in inventions than maintaining a business. He turned the company over to Hubbard, now his father-in-law. But thanks to Bell Telephone, he could enjoy financial security.

MORE SCIENTIFIC DISCOVERY

After Bell's marriage to Mabel in 1877, they moved to Washington, DC. Bell's lifelong curiosity led him from one project to another. He thought about transmitting voice without wires and the photophone. In 1880, he established the Volta Laboratory for scientific purposes. The next year, he connected the telephone with an induction device that together could serve as a metal detector. He tried to find the location of a bullet lodged in President Garfield's body during an assassination attempt. But the staff ignored Bell's instructions to move Garfield off his bed of metal springs. Bell's device could only detect static. Had the staff listened, this probe could have possibly found the bullet and removed it. Garfield might have lived.

A US citizen since 1882, Bell became one of the founders of the National Geographic Society in 1888. He started the American Association to Promote Teaching of Speech to the Deaf in 1890. He explored flight and in 1907 started the Aerial Experiment Association, which developed several flying machines and hydrofoils.

FACING ADVERSITY

Bell's ideas were repeatedly challenged. He also faced the failure of his school and the loss of a child. In a trial with the Pan-Electric Company over telephony patents, he was accused of bribery and corruption. The Bell Company, which later became American

James A. Garfield was sworn in as the twentieth US president on March 4, 1881. No one knew then that he would only serve for six months or that his bullet wounds would allow Bell to test his metal detector.

Telephone & Telegraph (AT&T), won the trial. Edward Gallaudet, the inventor of sign language, fought against Bell so severely that he had Bell unlicensed as a teacher of the deaf. Bell's methods focused on lip reading and speech therapy. In response to Gallaudet, Bell founded his own association of teachers for the deaf.

By the summer of 1885, the Bells decided they needed a refuge, a place to escape the pressures of their daily lives. They found such a place at Cape Breton Island in Canada's Newfoundland. Bell spent his last years attending events that marked the birth of the telephone. He died on Cape Breton Island in 1922. The entire telephone system came to a halt for a full minute to honor him. Bell may not have considered himself a businessman, but he was an entrepreneur whose visions came from his early life in Scotland.

CHAPTER 4

AN WANG'S INVESTMENT PAYS OFF

An Wang's name may not be well known outside the Boston area, but he stands out as an important immigrant entrepreneur. Born in Shanghai in 1920, his name means "peaceful king."[1] He was the eldest of five children.

THE SON OF AN ENGLISH TEACHER

An's father, Yun-Lu Wang, taught English in a private school. He was far more educated than most Chinese at the time, even though he just completed one year of university. An enjoyed a middle-class upbringing and began to learn English from his father at age four. The school where his father taught had no kindergarten or first grade. When An turned six and was ready for school, he was placed in the third grade. He was two years younger than his classmates and continued to be for the rest of his time there. Although it was difficult, he fought to keep up. Early on he discovered his talent for math. He did not perform well in other subjects but believed in himself anyway. When he took a test to enter junior high school, he scored higher than all the other applicants. He began reading a lot, as books gave

Chinese American computer entrepreneur An Wang is shown here with an early computer produced by Wang Laboratories in 1979.

him a window into the world beyond China. He particularly liked reading about Sir Isaac Newton, Leonardo da Vinci, and Galileo.

He entered Shanghai Provincial High School, one of the best schools in China. But not long after he enrolled, the school moved ten miles (sixteen kilometers) outside Shanghai, so An had to live at the school to remain a student. As a result, he never knew his siblings very well. Still, he knew he came from a respected family. He also didn't take life for granted because political conflicts and violence often broke out in Shanghai because of its location at the mouth of the Yangtze River, which led to inland China.

Shanghai has a waterfront section along the Huangpu River, shown here in 1998. It is one of the world's most populous cities. Shanghai has been called the "Pearl of the Orient" and "Paris of the East."

ON TO UNIVERSITY

At sixteen, he entered Shanghai's Chiao Tung University and studied electrical engineering and communications. His entrance scores, the highest of all members of his class, qualified him to serve as class president. His schoolwork came to him easily, allowing him time to play table tennis and edit a science journal. War constantly threatened his college years as the Japanese invaded China. After summer vacation between his freshman and sophomore years, only fifteen of the thirty students in his class returned, and his school moved again for safety.[2]

45

WAR'S NECESSITY IS THE MOTHER OF INVENTION

He graduated from college in 1940 and spent a year as a teaching assistant in electrical engineering. Then Wang decided he should contribute to the war effort. He and some of his classmates designed and built radios and transmitters for the Chinese government. Later, Wang designed a generator, giving him a taste of entrepreneurial success. Toward the end of the war he heard about a program to send talented engineers to the United States for additional training that would help rebuild China. Wang saw an opportunity and took the entrance exam. He placed second, excited to train abroad. The program accepted several hundred engineers. In April 1945, Wang flew to America, the first flight of his life, for what he thought would be a two-year visit.

When Wang arrived, he had a small amount of money and knowledge of both engineering and English. He had never experienced racial prejudice or discrimination that would prevent him from achieving his goals. He waited to learn what his two-year assignment would be and thought about pursuing an advanced degree. He'd heard of Harvard in China, as the chair of his university's electrical engineering department had studied there. He applied

Wang's future boss at the Harvard Computational Laboratory, mathematician Howard Aiken, is shown here in 1944 standing with his early computer to be used by the US Navy. In these early days of computing, the machinery took up entire rooms.

and was grateful that Chiao Tung University had an international reputation. In September 1945, he moved into a graduate student residency hall. Wang completed his master's degree the following year. He planned to return to China after his second year, but funding for his program ended because of civil war in China. He stayed at Harvard and, among other courses, studied digital electronic circuitry, which introduced him to computers. He completed his PhD, but his real research came afterward when he joined the Harvard Computational Laboratory in 1948 as a research fellow. At this time, there was only one operational computer in the whole country. His boss gave him a problem to solve regarding data storage. Wang mulled it over for three weeks. Then one day as he walked across Harvard Yard, he came up with a groundbreaking solution. It took much longer to find the right materials for his storage design: magnetic core memory. He had no idea he was making history. He viewed the solution as a gift and not as the result of thinking logically. It had come to him in a flash, out of nowhere.

By 1950, he considered working independently. He wanted to use his core memory solution for real-life problems. He did not know his invention would make him wealthy.

FROM RESEARCH FELLOW TO COMPUTING ENTREPRENEUR

In 1951, it was unusual for a researcher to start his own company. More likely he would join a large corporation. But Wang took the risk, which he considered to be small. He also got married to Lorraine Chiu. Like him, Chiu came from Shanghai and traveled to America to study in Massachusetts. He filed a patent and worked with Harvard administrators and legal experts to stake his claim. He noticed that

In this 1980 photo, Wang Cathode Ray Tube (CRT) terminals appear lined up for inspection and action in a final assembly room at the Wang Laboratories headquarters in Lowell, Massachusetts.

large companies were beginning to make computers and opened Wang Laboratories. He chose to include his name in the company's title because he wanted it to reflect his values. He found two hundred square feet (eighteen square meters) of office space in Boston for $600.[3] He had no furniture, no customers, and no orders. He started by buying a table and a chair and getting telephone service. He contacted everyone he knew at universities based on his earlier work on core memory. He borrowed a government directory from the Harvard library and started a letter writing campaign. He searched a list of proposal requests to see if he could work on the projects.

While he tried to grow his business, he also worked on his ideas for commercial application. Used to solving problems with paper and pencil, he took notes in loose-leaf notebooks. Within three weeks, he received his first order. He hired his first employee, a young man who had studied advertising. Wang was on his way.

He focused on digital electronics and developed a digital counting device. He experimented more with magnetic memory cores and logic circuits. His goal was to make life easier for scientists as they needed to count, store, and compute data. He also designed digital equipment for clients. Although he valued research and innovation, he did not believe in research for research's sake. Instead, he wanted his products to be helpful and solve problems.

His company produced calculators and then word processors and computers. It dominated the word-processing market by the end of the 1970s. During its heyday, Wang Laboratories products sold to more than 80 percent of America's two thousand largest companies. In 1994, Wang ranked as the fifth richest American, worth about $1.6 billion. His research led him to hold forty patents and twenty-three honorary degrees.[4]

AN IMMIGRANT ENTREPRENEUR GIVES NEW LIFE TO AN OLD TEXTILE TOWN

By the mid-1970s, Wang sought out a new location to expand his company's operations. The factory town of Lowell, Massachusetts, impressed him. He appreciated its history as an early industrial center, a planned city with canals and factories, named after businessman Francis Cabot Lowell. But the city had also been labeled as a failed city, unable to adapt to economic changes.

When Wang purchased the property in 1976, Lowell city officials were not pleased. They wanted to attract a larger, more well known company. But after relocating to Lowell, the company grew tremendously, leading city officials to change their minds.

Over time, Wang Laboratories occupied more than two million square feet (185,806 sq meters) and the Lowell unemployment rate dropped from 15 to 3 percent.[5] The company worked together with the city to build a new Hilton hotel that would provide lodging for Wang employees in training. For this, Wang relocated his training center from Burlington, Massachusetts, to Lowell. The move secured the money necessary for construction.

Wang Laboratories received recognition for its contributions to the "Massachusetts Miracle," which describes how high-technology companies brought new life to old factory towns.[6]

BIG BLUE CHALLENGES WANG

The success of Wang Laboratories brought out the competition, none more so than the computing giant IBM. Wang allowed IBM to license his core memory patent for $400,000[7] and never looked back. He always believed Wang Laboratories could overtake IBM.

But competitors weren't Wang's only challenge. In 1982, Wang announced his retirement and turned over control of the company to his son, Fred. Although Fred had graduated from business school, he lacked his father's vison or business skills. Wang had to fire and replace his own son in 1989.

LESSONS FROM AN WANG

In 1986, An Wang and coauthor Eugene Linden published *Lessons: An Autobiography*. In the book, Wang describes his path from Shanghai to New England and how he started a $2.3 billion company from the ground up. His lessons include:

Don't let anyone or anything get to you.
Don't let outside forces influence your company.
If they do, don't admit it, even to yourself.
Mistakes happen.
Risk failure to move forward.[8]

AN WANG'S LEGACY

Wang never expected to become as wealthy as he did. He never lost sight of his roots and the people who helped him. His philanthropic activities were numerous. He donated millions in funds to his alma mater, Harvard University, and to his wife's alma mater, Wellesley College. He also provided money to build a factory in Boston's Chinatown that provided jobs for three hundred inner-city workers. With $4 million, he helped build a new roof for Boston's Metropolitan Center, now known as the Wang Center for the Performing Arts. With $6 million, he created the Wang Institute of Graduate Studies for software engineers and China scholars.[9]

Wang died of esophageal cancer in 1990. Although Wang Laboratories no longer exists, Wang's name lives on through his patents and philanthropy.

CHAPTER 5

ANDY GROVE: FROM REFUGEE TO THRIVING BUSINESSMAN

Andy Grove was born in 1936 to a Jewish dairyman and a bookkeeping clerk in Budapest, Hungary. His birth name was András István Gróf. As a boy, Andy quickly became a survivor. At age four, he bounced back from a case of scarlet fever, but for the rest of his life he suffered the results of a middle-ear infection.

ESCAPING NAZISM, THEN COMMUNISM

After Budapest's scarlet fever outbreak, a new plague overcame Hungary and the rest of Europe: Nazi Germany. In 1941, Andy's father simply disappeared after being rounded up for a work crew. Signs appeared in Budapest shops announcing they did not sell to Jews. Andy and his mother went into hiding. As young as he was, he knew something bad was happening. His mother told him he would have a different name, a Christian name, András Malesevics.

Intel CEO Andy Grove poses in Palo Alto, California, the heart of Silicon Valley, for this portrait in 2000.

After the war, his father miraculously returned from the Eastern Front, yet he was only a shadow of the father Andy remembered. Andy wanted to make his parents proud so he focused on his education and getting into college. At twelve, he fell in love with journalism while working on a youth newspaper. But when his journalist uncle got into legal trouble, Andy's articles were rejected. He decided not to involve himself in an occupation that could be so slanted. He found safety in science, especially chemistry. His natural curiosity distinguished him, but he was not a typical bookworm. He engaged in sports and singing. He loved opera and dreamed of one day becoming an opera singer.

The Russians liberated Budapest and Hungary in 1945. But there was a dark side, too. One of the Russian soldiers raped Andy's mother. The Soviets replaced Nazi occupation with Stalinist dictatorship. Teased at school for being a Jew and the son of a dairyman, Andy decided he wasn't going to live under a Soviet regime. He and his best friend took a train close to the Austrian border. After news spread of Russian invasions and police checkpoints, the boys pooled their money together and bought back-road directions from a smuggler. Lying facedown in the mud hours later, he heard a voice yell in Hungarian, "Who is there?" Andy thought he would be killed in this moment. He answered, "Where are we?" The voice said, "Austria."[1]

They were safe.

A REFRESHING CHANGE

Grove was now a refugee, along with thousands of other Hungarians. With the help of the International Rescue Committee (IRC), he made his way from Vienna to the United States in the winter of 1956–57. The IRC gave him a blank check to buy the best hearing aid he could find. Used to being criticized for one reason or another, he found New York

Anti-Semitic signs, like this 1933 sign in Berlin, Germany, urging the public to avoid Jewish doctors and lawyers, made it difficult for Jewish families like Grove's to earn a living and survive.

City to be a nice change. He stayed with an aunt and uncle in Brooklyn and entered City College of New York, which at the time offered free tuition. He graduated in 1960 with a degree in chemical engineering, and his professors remarked on his drive and ambition. They knew they

THE HUNGARIAN REVOLUTION

As World War II ended, Soviet Russia took control of Hungary. Thousands of troops and hundreds of tanks appeared. Although the Hungarians believed there would be some relief after Soviet dictator Josef Stalin died in 1953, his successor forced Mátyás Rákosi, the Hungarian prime minister appointed by Stalin, to resign. On October 23, 1956, students (among them the young András István Gróf) and laborers issued a list of demands, including freedom for the individual, more food, and removal of both the secret police and Russian control. They released this list issued to newly appointed prime minister Imre Nagy. They dismantled a large statue of Stalin. The Red Army pulled out, but the victory was short-lived.

On November 4, Soviets returned to Budapest with tanks to restore order. Within ten days, the Soviets regained control but not without thousands of Hungarian deaths. US president Eisenhower tripled the immigration quota to allow more Hungarian refugees to enter America. Some forty thousand Hungarians from all parts of the country escaped by train and on foot into Austria where they received aid in refugee camps and journeyed to America by liberty ships or American military aircraft.[2] Many of these were young people who left their parents and siblings behind in search of a future free of tyranny.

would hear more about him one day. At City College, Grove crossed out the Hungarian name no one could pronounce and replaced it with Andrew Stephen Grove. He would become known as Andy.

Brooklyn, New York, has long been home to a variety of immigrant groups. Grove would have likely seen this intersection of Fulton Street and Flatbush Avenue, one of the longest streets in this New York City borough, shown here in 1948.

While in college, Grove married a refugee, Eva Kastan, whom he met while working at a New Hampshire resort one summer. After his graduation, they decided to move to California, and Grove became a doctoral student at the University of California at Berkeley. He excelled at his studies once again, and when he finished his PhD in chemical engineering in 1963, he had his pick of employers. He narrowed his list down to two research groups: Bell Laboratories or Fairchild Semiconductor, a start-up. He checked around and according to what he heard around Berkeley, he chose Fairchild.

Fairchild suited him. Other brilliant engineers surrounded him there, and they all tried to figure out how to make the early computers of the 1960s process information faster. Gordon Moore, who headed up research at Fairchild, thought an integrated circuit made of silicon could provide the answer. Grove, though, had a background in fluid dynamics and knew nothing about integrated circuits. On the job, he was asked to examine the electrical characteristics of a particular kind of transistor. He delivered an impressive report. Grove and a couple of colleagues worked to make silicon usable. They found that sodium was the problem. Grove and his team won an industry award, and Eva realized she'd married no ordinary Hungarian man. But no one at Fairchild seemed to care that Grove had made this miraculous discovery.

JUMPING SHIP

By 1968, Grove saw no future for himself at Fairchild. The company just didn't understand the semiconductor business. When his bosses Robert Noyce and Gordon Moore decided to leave, Grove joined them. Together, they formed Integrated Electronics, or Intel for short, in Mountain View, California. The early years were not easy, because the industry was changing so rapidly. Grove called it a pressure cooker.[3]

Grove's Intel became a microchip phenomenon. It attracted the best technological minds to its Santa Clara, California, headquarters. The no-photos sign on the gate is to ensure the company's operations and its trade secrets remain protected.

At age thirty-two, he was in charge of the company's operations. He was expected to manage, but he didn't even know what the word meant. He read a magazine article about how movie directors had to have great vision and pull all the elements together to make it reality. It dawned on him that this was the job he needed to do at Intel.

The company introduced its first microchip in 1977. Moore took the young Grove under his wing and nurtured him. Moore told him one day he'd run Intel and in 1979, Grove became president. When Moore stepped down as CEO in 1987, Grove followed him. He became chairman of the company in 1997 and served until 2005. Both Moore and Grove conducted their business from cubicles, just like everyone else. And thousands of the company's employees became millionaires.

Grove ran the company with an iron fist. He did not put up with lateness or mistakes. He earned a reputation as a tough leader and was recognized in 1984 in *Fortune* magazine as one of America's toughest.[4] His leadership style did push away some valued managers in a way that even a sincere apology could not fix. At the same time, the style helped Intel navigate some rough waters that included weak demand for product, flawed product, increased competition, and production problems.

Some angry customers called the media when a flawed chip emerged in 1994. Grove beat himself up about it and developed a plan to make things right. He decided the company would replace the millions of flawed Pentium chips even if company representatives had to deliver in-home service. It was a risky move, but one that brought great benefits. Intel became a household brand.

Just like Grove himself, Intel survived disaster after disaster. He was praised as an innovator and teacher in the high-tech industry. He made the impossible happen, or so it seemed. He made risky moves like shelving a product Intel started, causing great disruption. His business strategies inspired authors to write about him. Under Grove's leadership, Intel grew to sixty-four thousand employees.[5] All of Silicon Valley felt his influence. He shared his business insights by authoring two books: *High Output Management* (1983) and *Only the Paranoid Survive* (1996).

Grove wanted to get involved in the Stanford Graduate School of Business. The school was eager to accept his offer and have an active CEO engage with its MBA students. Together they created a class in strategy and action in the information processing industry. As a teacher, just as a manager, Grove searched for answers and opinions. Students valued their one-on-one time with him. Grove was still a student himself, always looking for opportunities to improve himself.

ONLY THE PARANOID SURVIVE

In 1996, Grove published *Only the Paranoid Survive: How to Exploit the Crisis Points That Challenge Every Company and Career.* Certainly Grove knew about crisis, both personally and professionally. He told readers to keep looking over their shoulders, because technology changes so much that colleagues can easily turn into competitors. He called moments of crisis that demand decision "strategic inflection points." For Intel, such points included the transition from memory chips to microprocessors. Throughout the book's nine chapters, Grove as a dedicated business teacher shares his business wisdom:

- Sooner or later, something important in business will change.
- New rules will take over.
- Transitions change business and how companies manage transition determines their future.
- The basis of both computing and competition has changed.
- Debate brings clarity.
- Experimentation leads to solutions.
- Transformation demands clarity of direction.[6]

But in 1994, Grove discovered he had a tumor. He was diagnosed with prostate cancer.

TACKLING CANCER AND PHILANTHROPY

With the same strength Grove applied to his academic studies years before, he tackled cancer. He underwent cutting-edge radiation treatment and wrote a magazine cover story about it in 1996. At the same time, he and Eva tried to figure out what to do with all of their wealth. They lived modestly. They funded chemistry scholarships at City College of New York and established the Grove School of Engineering at City College of New York. Grove donated funds to prostate cancer research and the IRC. In 1997, *Time* magazine anointed Grove its Man of the Year.[7] When later diagnosed with Parkinson's disease, he contributed millions to research and again took to the pages of business magazines to lobby for research.

He published *Swimming Across: A Memoir* in 2001. Grove died at age seventy-nine of cancer. His obituaries and tributes praised him as an immigrant survivor who created Silicon Valley.

CHAPTER 6

ARIANNA HUFFINGTON NAVIGATES HER WAY TO MEDIA MOGUL

Born 1950 in Athens, Greece, Ariadne Stassino-poulou was the daughter of a journalist and a management consultant. She moved with her mother to England at age sixteen. There, she attended Cambridge University. She headed up its famous debate society, the Cambridge Union, and graduated with a master's degree in economics. She pursued writing in London, and in 1974 published her first book, *The Female Woman*. It explored trends in women's liberation movements. A writer with a political bent, she then authored *After Reason* in 1978. This book criticized the lack of soul in the media.

Ever mindful of the media, Greek immigrant entrepreneur Arianna Huffington posed for the cameras at a New York City photographer's studio in 1988.

65

Opera soprano Maria Callas, whom Huffington profiled in a 2002 book, was born in New York City to Greek parents. Her vocal range earned her fame and fortune. She died at age fifty-three from a heart attack.

THE MOVE TO THE UNITED STATES

After a failed romance in London with a *Times* columnist, Huffington moved to New York City in 1980. She continued to write, this time a biography of one of the world's most famous opera singers, Maria Callas, also of Greek ancestry. Critics loved the book, so Huffington decided to continue writing about her heritage. In *The Gods of Greece*, she wrote about ancient Greek myths. She then turned to another biography, this time of Spanish painter Pablo Picasso. She was accused of plagiarism in writing her two biographies.[1]

While writing, the young Greek immigrant met billionaire oilman Michael Huffington, a secretary in the US Department of Defense. They married in 1986 and moved to Santa Barbara, California. Huffington became a US citizen in 1990 and gave birth to two daughters. Her husband became a congressman, serving from 1993 to 1995. She supported his Senate campaign that followed, but he lost. The campaign, however, allowed her to gain media attention, and she rose in fame. The couple divorced in 1997. A year later, Michael Huffington announced he was bisexual.

By now Huffington was known for her conservative political views. She began appearing on television to make

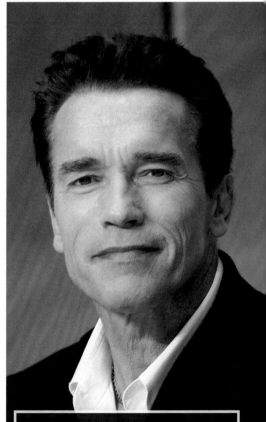

Austrian Arnold Schwarzenegger came to America as an immigrant and bodybuilder in 1968 at age twenty-one. He became an action film star and California governor. Huffington ran against him in 2003.

her opinions known. Eventually, she leaned more toward ecology and corporate reform. In 2003, she campaigned on an independent ticket against Arnold Schwarzenegger for California governor. She withdrew from the race to support incumbent Governor Gray Davis. But throughout her political pursuits, she kept writing. In 2003, her book *Pigs at the Trough: How Corporate Greed and Political Corruption Are Undermining America* became a *New York Times* bestseller.

EMPRESS OF THE MEDIA

Huffington took her politics to the Internet. She launched a website, Resignation.com, to rail against Democratic president Bill Clinton. Huffington created a new kind of media platform in 2005 when she launched the Huffington Post with Kenneth Lerer. She became the editor in chief. At first, the website offered blog posts, liberal politics, and news aggregation. It grew to address a wide range of topics and within three years, it became the most powerful blog in the world. It uses a network of thousands of unpaid bloggers. In 2010, it reported revenues of $30 million, mostly from advertising on the website.[2]

The Huffington Post, shown here, created a new kind of internet journalism that allows a greater number of content creators. It proved that the news can come from a variety of places and viewpoints.

The Huffington Post brought Huffington the kind of fame she craved to serve her own media interests. She became host of at least two national public radio programs. But her politics seemed to move with the tides, and her changing views sparked backlash. Still, she is the queen of spin, of finding a way of angling a story to meet her needs.

As the Huffington Post successfully grew, Huffington continued to pursue her personal writing. In 2007, she published a self-help book, *On Becoming Fearless…in Love, Work, and Life*. It later inspired a Huffington Post blog series.

Huffington became a household name, appearing on *Time* magazine's list of the one hundred most influential people in the world.[3] She also made the list of *Forbes* magazine's World's 100 Most Powerful Women.[4] One of her staff writers won a Pulitzer Prize, making the Huffington Post a prize-winning platform. But the Huffington Post required cash to continue its success. Since it was not a great moneymaker, nor was it intended to be, the funding had to come from somewhere.

SELLING THE HUFFINGTON POST

In a controversial move, Huffington sold her website to AOL in 2011 for upwards of $300 million.[5] Huffington had met AOL chief executive officer Tim Armstrong at a digital media conference. It was a sweet deal for her. She had not invested any of her money in the Huffington Post. Now she pocketed $21 million from the sale[6] and assumed the title of president and editor in chief of the Huffington Post Media Group. This position also included oversight of AOL's news operations, including the Patch news service, the MapQuest navigation website, Moviefone, and TechCrunch, a site that profiles start-ups, reviews new technology products, and shares breaking news in the technology industry. AOL needed her to pump some life into its struggling news service, but the Huffington Post was barely profitable. With revenues of $31 million, it only produced a $1 million profit.[7] Huffington's projected profits after the sale did not come to be. The only real profitable year the Huffington Post had was in 2011, the year of the sale.

Although she wanted to change the face of journalism, she couldn't make it work. Several initiatives she launched at AOL met with failure. Her critics believed she saw herself as more capable than she was. These critics also maintained that the purpose of the Huffington Post was not about journalism but about the ego and position of Arianna Huffington. Huffington refused to pay any attention to the naysayers.

Armstrong provided Huffington with a generous budget and she hired top journalistic talent. She opened Huffington Post news bureaus around the world and expanded the number of areas the Post would cover. Her critics, again, complained about her spending. The combination of excessive spending and not hitting her projected financial targets began to trouble Armstrong. While she excelled at reaching out to people, often giving audiences her personal email address and responding to their messages, she did not ask for help when she was out of her comfort zone. She thought about separating her company from AOL. Armstrong would let her off the hook if she could find a buyer for $1 billion,[8] but no buyer came forth. Armstrong put an AOL executive in place to help control costs and he took the AOL news properties out of Huffington's control.

Huffington tried a new strategy for news. She wanted to focus on positive news and not just report on negative events. The shift did not go over well with her staff. Meanwhile, Armstrong was increasingly cutting her out of day-to-day operations. By May 2015, he was close to selling AOL to telecommunications giant Verizon. At a press conference with Verizon and Armstrong, neither Huffington nor the Huffington Post was mentioned. To make matters worse, interest in the Huffington Post was fading because of competitors such as BuzzFeed, led by Huffington's former investor, Lerer. He helped her start the Huffington Post.

THE HUFFINGTON POST INTRODUCES AND THEN MODIFIES A NEW MODEL

Arianna Huffington's brainchild uses a network of thousands of unpaid writers. This new model changed what was considered journalism. It published about one hundred original posts each day, both paid and unpaid, and that's just in the politics section. The unpaid bloggers are citizen journalists, everyday people with something to say. Their posts generate comments and site traffic, and that entices advertisers, from whom the company collects money.

The Huffington model has been likened to a ship powered by galley slaves and led by pirates. Using unpaid bloggers gave Huffington a way to scale up and build an enormous audience quickly. In lieu of pay, the website offered exposure and influence. But in 2015, the network had more than a million contributors, and changes needed to be made. The company introduced a content management system named Athena after the Greek goddess of wisdom. Now bloggers can post directly to the site.

However, Athena has forced many bloggers to reconsider posting. Their posts now have to be featured. They find they have to promote their Huffington Post blog posts on their own social media or other sites. The blog posts are no longer appearing in special news sections, such as politics, but appear only under the blog, where they are not indexed, meaning they won't come up in a Google search.

Huffington stayed at AOL for four years and then stepped down to launch Thrive Global, a company and web platform to promote health and wellness. After a collapse from exhaustion two years after launching the Huffington Post, she gained inspiration to write about balancing health and work.

PUBLIC WORKS

Huffington has contributed her time to serve on two boards of community organizations. A Place Called Home serves at-risk children in South Los Angeles. She is a former trustee of Los Angeles' Archer School for Girls, a prep school that her two daughters attended. She has also been a speaker at the World Economic Summit for several years.

40 PERCENT OF IMMIGRANT ENTREPRENEURS ARE WOMEN

According to the National Council of Business Women, 40 percent of immigrant entrepreneurs are women.[9] And according to *Forbes*, 30 percent of the fifty most successful self-made women are immigrants.[10] One such woman is Thai Lee, born in Thailand, the daughter of a Korean economist. She moved to the United States as a teenager and received degrees from Amherst College and the Harvard Business School. She is now CEO of SHI International, a provider of information technology products and services. She

(continued on the next page)

(continued from the previous page)

and her husband bought the business for $1 million in 1989 and have expanded it into a $7.5 billion global business.[11]

Here are some other examples of female immigrant entrepreneurs:

- Neerja Sethi, born in India, is vice president of corporate affairs and a director of Syntel, a New York City–based information technology consulting firm. She and her husband, Bharat Desai, founded the company in 1980 from their Troy, Michigan, apartment with $2,000.[12]
- Fashion icon and designer Diane von Furstenberg was born in Belgium. She came to the United States in 1970 and founded her company, DVF. She created the popular wrap dress that sold one million units within two years.[13]
- Peggy Cherng, born in Burma, cofounded the Chinese fast-food chain Panda Express. She gave up her software career to join her husband's family business. They started in Glendale, California, and now have some two thousand locations.[14]
- Born in Morocco, Sonia Gardner cofounded Avenue Capital with her brother, Marc Lasry. Four years before they founded an investment brokerage firm, Amroc Investments.[15]

Huffington has proved that she adapts to her situations. Where she sees opportunity, she grabs it. She doesn't let anyone tell her she can't do something. She has written fifteen books since 1973. Her 2014 book, *Thrive: The Third Metric to Redefining Success and Creating a Life of Well-Being*, debuted on the top spot of the *New York Times* bestseller list.

CHAPTER 7

VINOD KHOSLA MENTORS NEW ENTREPRENEURS

Vinod Khosla was born in Delhi, India, in 1955. He grew up dreaming of becoming an entrepreneur. At fourteen, he heard about Intel starting up. The news reached India about a year after the event. He wanted to start his own company and throughout his early years, Intel served as a role model for him. He earned a bachelor's degree in electrical engineering from the Indian Institute of Technology in New Delhi. He tried to start a soy milk company to help those in India without refrigerators. He thought soy milk, which doesn't require refrigeration, could be a substitute for dairy milk. But he was twenty and had no money. His idea failed.

Indian immigrant entrepreneur Vinod Khosla poses in Menlo Park, California, in 2006. Khosla has translated his business experience into helping other entrepreneurs realize their own dreams.

75

BUSINESS SUCCESS IN THE UNITED STATES

Khosla came to America to study biomedical engineering—the field he'd trained for in India. He received his master's degree in biomedical engineering on a full scholarship from Carnegie Mellon University in Pittsburgh, Pennsylvania. He believed this was the only way he could get somewhere.

Khosla had always planned to get his MBA at Stanford University and to become part of the legendary Silicon Valley culture. He applied to the school but was turned down. The administrators told him to get some work experience. In Pittsburgh, he did just that. He landed a few jobs and applied again but Stanford rejected him once more. He talked to the director of admissions. In fact, he yelled and screamed at him to place him on the waiting list. Khosla was not convinced he'd be admitted after applying a third time, so he also applied to Carnegie Mellon. He told himself he could go to business school in Pittsburgh, where he was accepted, and then go on to Silicon Valley. Yet, he didn't give up on Stanford. He got to know everyone in the admissions office. He spoke to the women there every day, and they became his supporters. He became friends with the admissions director, who sympathized but still wouldn't admit him. He was three weeks into the MBA program at Carnegie Mellon when he spoke to the Stanford admissions director yet again. He made a plea a few days before Stanford's registration for classes to let him come. He told the director he was leaving in the morning, and he'd be there the next day. Within twenty-four hours, the director told him that he could indeed come. From this experience, Khosla learned perseverance, the importance of selling his ideas, and of showing up. He knew these qualities would be important to his career as an entrepreneur.

IMMIGRANTS FROM INDIA AND PAKISTAN SPAWN INNOVATION

Among the top four hundred billionaires listed by *Forbes* magazine in 2016 are several born in India and Pakistan. Here are two of them:

Romesh Wadhwani, born in 1947 in an area now part of Pakistan, serves as chairman and CEO of Symphony Technology Group, a company he founded. Like Khosla, he studied at the Indian Institute of Technology and received a master's degree in electrical engineering at Carnegie Mellon University, where he also completed his doctorate. His career in business started immediately after graduation when he founded an industrial-controls company and later a software firm he sold for more than $9 billion in stock. Wadhwani received the 2013 Forbes India Non-Resident Philanthropist Award. He has since announced a commitment to fund $1 billion in India entrepreneur initiatives.[1]

John Kapoor was the first in his family to go to college. He came to the United States to get his doctorate in medicinal chemistry at the State University of New York in Buffalo. After graduation, he entered the corporate world. He founded Insys Therapeutics in 2002 and served as chairman until January 2017, when several company executives were arrested for bribing physicians to prescribe one of the company's cancer treatment drugs to patients without cancer. Kapoor ran several pharmaceutical outfits in his long career and became known for pushing the legal and ethical limits.[2] He serves as chairman of generic drug company Akorn. Outside the pharmaceutical industry, Kapoor also owns a chain of Roka Akor Japanese restaurants in Chicago; Scottsdale, Arizona; and San Francisco.

In previous years, Vinod Khosla held positions on this list.[3]

A GENUINE SILICON VALLEY BUSINESSMAN

Khosla arrived at Stanford with no place to stay. The office workers with whom he'd made friends put him up for his first month. He'd made it to Stanford and Silicon Valley. He received his MBA in 1980. Immediately afterward, Khosla cofounded Daisy Systems, a major computer-aided design (CAD) system for electrical engineers. Bothered by the lack of hardware, in 1982 he cofounded Sun (Stanford University Network) Microsystems, which produced workstations for software developers. For one week, the company was named Sun Workstations. But no one knew then what a workstation—an office with a computer or computer terminal—even was.

Khosla was a pioneer of the open systems that allowed developers to work together. His friend John Doerr, a board member of venture capital firm Kleiner Perkins Caufield and Byers (KPCB), funded the company. Khosla served as founding CEO and chairman from 1982 to 1984. But he then joined KPCB in 1986.

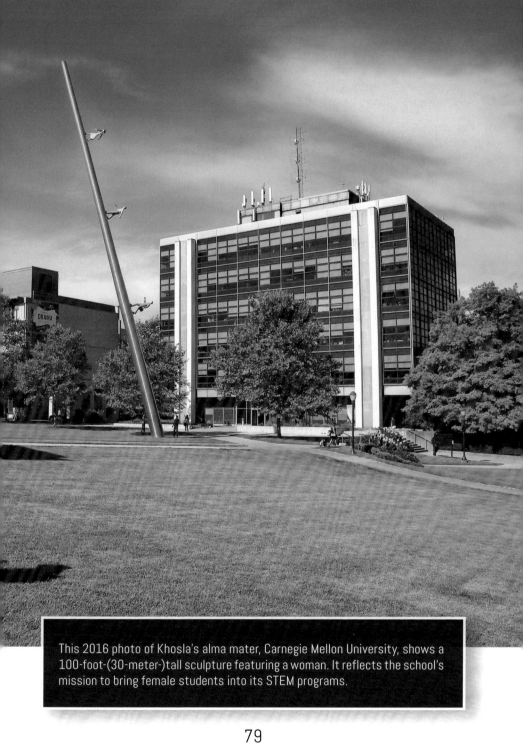

This 2016 photo of Khosla's alma mater, Carnegie Mellon University, shows a 100-foot-(30-meter-)tall sculpture featuring a woman. It reflects the school's mission to bring female students into its STEM programs.

He found as a venture capitalist he could help level the playing field. For example, he challenged Intel's market lead in the processor sector with Nexgen/Advanced Micro Systems (AMD). He also challenged Cisco System's lead in the router market with Juniper Networks. One of the projects he funded was for Andy Bechtolsheim, his Sun Microsystems cofounder. Bechtolsheim left Sun in 1987 and wanted to use Sun's technology to create a general-purpose workstation. It turned out to be a profitable investment and successful product.

ENTREPRENEURIAL POWER CHANGES WHAT IS POSSIBLE

Khosla predicted the changes that would come to long-distance telephone companies. He imagined the calls would be free and said so in 1996. At the time, long distance represented most of AT&T's revenues. His prediction proved correct, because at the core, Khosla believes that technology redefines the very meaning of possibility. To him, entrepreneurial ideas drive the future.

By 2004, he launched his own venture capital firm, Khosla Ventures. With this company's resources, he helps entrepreneurs build new energy and technology companies that make a difference. He is known for his hope and vision. He is particularly interested in funding companies that offer technology for ecological improvements. One of these companies was KiOR. But in 2014 it filed for bankruptcy with more than two thousand creditors left without their money, including the state of Mississippi. Stakeholders, including Khosla Ventures, had to make up for the costly loss. But Khosla continues to believe in American technology.

"The combination of brilliant ideas and entrepreneurial spirit should lead us to a safer and more secure future,"[4] he said in 2007. Plus, his firm has invested in several biofuel technologies, and capital-seeking entrepreneurs continue to pursue his investment.

Khosla believes in Moore's law about the rate of technology change, based on Intel's Gordon Moore's observation that the number of transistors on an integrated circuit doubles every two years. He believes that this law could apply to biofuels, too. But his critics wonder how well a Silicon Valley attitude will play out in the oil industry. Some argue that Khosla has done more harm than good.

RISK LEADS TO SUCCESS

Khosla has found that he has to defend himself and his investment decisions. His Silicon Valley training taught him that business risk is expected, as is failure. Without them, success is not possible. He said that he expects half the companies Khosla Ventures invests in to actually make money. "New industries are created by entrepreneurs who don't necessarily have subject matter expertise when they get started, yet they are still responsible for most of the innovation we see in society,"[5] he told CBS's *60 Minutes*.

He brought himself into the argument, questioning what he knew about computing when he founded Sun Microsystems. Yet his lack of knowledge didn't end his goals. He advises budding entrepreneurs to be wary of experts, because experts may have no direct experience in a start-up. He also cautions against reliance on spreadsheets, because a savvy analyst knows how to manipulate the numbers. He believes it helps to be naïve and to have great imagination.

Khosla knows a thing or two about persistence. At Sun Microsystems, a major customer hinted it was going to buy from a major competitor. Khosla took a red-eye flight from California to the East Coast and waited in the customer's lobby until the company's CEO agreed to meet with him. It was clear the CEO expected Khosla to just go away, but he persisted. He walked away the next day with a handwritten agreement. He doesn't believe in taking no for an answer without putting up a fight. He also maintains that truly believing in something can make it happen. He told an audience of Stanford business students, "I like to say my willingness to fail is what gives me the ability to succeed."[6]

THE KHOSLA LEGACY

Khosla believes in paying it forward. He serves as a founding board member of the Indian School of Business and as a charter member of the Indus Entrepreneurs, a nonprofit network of entrepreneurs with more than forty chapters in nine countries. He also signed a Giving Pledge, committing to donate half his wealth to charity. But unlike other philanthropists, Khosla does not rely on nonprofit organizations. He believes commercial organizations can better bring people out

KHOSLA AND SOCIAL ENTREPRENEURSHIP

While at KPCB, Khosla spoke about social entrepreneurship. It's a way to invest money in social or cultural change. Khosla pointed out an example to Stanford business students. He ran into a graduate who started a company selling hand- and foot-operated pumps to some twenty thousand customers in Kenya.[7] Khosla continues to practice these investment strategies to help the world become a better place. He uses microfinance as a way to erase poverty in India and Africa. This is a way of providing funding to low-income people and projects that would not ordinarily qualify for funding. Khosla is also experimenting with new ideas in education and global housing.

of poverty. He joined forces with other investors in 2013 to start a venture capital fund, Unitus Seed Fund, whose Unitus Labs promises to help some 800 million low-income people in India through Indian start-up ventures for consumer services.[8]

Venture capital and other investments can help impoverished parts of India and their people, such as those shown here barefoot and living on the street in Mumbai.

Khosla and his wife, Neeru, however, did start a nonprofit dedicated to STEM education. Nearly forty thousand schools use the foundation's resources.

In 2014, *Forbes* named Khosla to its list of smartest technology investors. Behind it all is a belief system Khosla follows, no matter what. He thinks about using technology to automate health care and for solving massive problems such as education and climate change. The chance to solve some of the world's greatest problems by funding start-up companies keeps Khosla going.

CHAPTER 8

SERGEY BRIN GOOGLES HIS WAY TO BILLIONAIRE

Sergey Mikhailovich Brin was born in Moscow, USSR (now Russia), in 1973. His father, Michael, was a professor of mathematics and his mother, Eugenia, a scientist. Yet, as Jews, they were denied career advancement and other opportunities. Michael faced anti-Semitism constantly. He wanted to become an astronomer and study at the university, but he was denied admission. There were quota systems by nationality, and Jews had to indicate their nationality as Jews. Further, Jews could not pursue certain sciences for fear they would leak nuclear secrets. Instead of physics, Michael decided on math and attended Moscow State University. He graduated in 1970 with honors and took a position with GOSPLAN, the state planning committee of the USSR, as an economist. With support from advisers, he obtained his doctorate at the University of Kharkiv.

Eugenia also attended Moscow State University. She studied math and mechanics. She worked in a research laboratory at the Soviet Oil and Gas Institute. The couple lived in a tiny three-room apartment.

Into this educated family Sergey Brin was born.

Russian immigrant Sergey Brin supports Google in many ways, including testing its products. In 2012, he wore Google Glass during New York City's Fashion Week. The product allows consumers to use a computer embedded into eyeglasses.

AMERICA AND A BETTER FUTURE

Brin's parents believed that the Soviet Union offered little for their son. After he attended a conference in Warsaw, Poland, in 1977, Michael decided it was time for the family to leave the USSR. He applied for an exit visa in the fall of 1978. As payback, he was fired from his job. Eugenia, too, was forced to give up her position. During the next few months, life became more and more difficult. Michael became a technical translator and used the time to teach himself computer programming. Finally, they received their exit visas and left for Vienna, Austria. There, they met members of the Hebrew Immigrant Aid Society, an organization that had helped Jewish immigrants come to America since the 1880s. The Brins moved on to Paris and stayed for a while. Michael found a research job. Finally in October 1979, Michael,

New York's John F. Kennedy International Airport has been the destination for many immigrants. The Emma Lazarus poem with the famous lines "Give me your tired, your poor, your huddled masses yearning to breathe free" is engraved in marble at the airport

Eugenia, Sergey, and Michael's mother landed at JFK Airport in Queens, New York. They had finally made it to the land of opportunity.

The Brins settled into a lower-middle-class neighborhood in Maryland. With a loan from the Jewish community, they were able to buy a car. Because Michael had earned his advanced degrees in the Soviet Union, respected for its mathematical training, he easily found an academic position at the University of Maryland. Eugenia also found a job at the National Aeronautics and Space Administration (NASA).

THE STUDENT YEARS IN MARYLAND

Sergey's introduction to the American school system actually began at the religious level. He attended the Mishkan Torah Hebrew School. But the kids there bullied him because of his thick Russian accent. He begged his parents for other options. They chose a Montessori elementary school in Adelphi. The Montessori method focused on peer learning

A young Brin used the Commodore 64 computer, pictured at the Gadget Show Live 2015 in Birmingham, England. Today it may seem primitive, but it sold more than ten million units and appears in the *Guinness Book of World Records*.

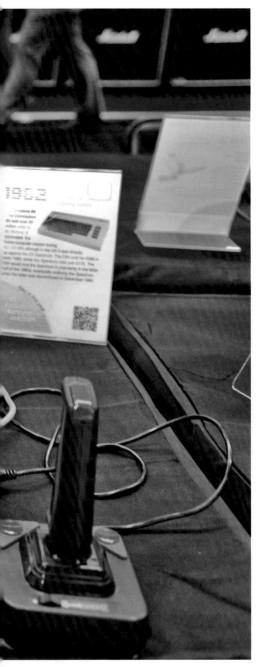

and developing a child not only intellectually, but also physically, socially, and emotionally.

Sergey blossomed and later named the school as a key reason for his success.[2] The school's director also became a friend of the family and Sergey's mentor. In school, numbers fascinated Sergey. But because he had advanced skills and his parents helped teach him at home, he grew bored in class. The chance to get his own personal computer delighted him. His father presented him with a Commodore 64 for his ninth birthday. Brin had no problem impressing his teachers with school projects done on his computer, delivering the results on computer printouts.

He attended Eleanor Roosevelt High School in Greenbelt for three years and was accepted into the University of Maryland at age fifteen in 1990. He graduated three years later with a double major in computer systems and mathematics. He received honors as well as a National Science Foundation Graduate Fellowship.

JEWISH REFUGEES ESCAPE SOVIET PERSECUTION

The year of Brin's emigration, 1979, marked the peak year of Jewish emigration from the Soviet Union—a rate of four thousand a month[1], just before the 1980 Olympics in Moscow. (The United States boycotted the event because of the USSR's invasion of Afghanistan.) Refugees typically traveled first to Vienna and during the wave of emigration in which the Brins participated, the Hebrew Immigrant Aid Society and the American Jewish Joint Distribution Committee helped them to the United States. Prior waves of refugees were led to Israel. Many Jews in the Soviet Union had come to realize that because of anti-Semitism and poor economic conditions, it was not a place to raise their children. Although the majority chose the United States as their destination, some also chose Australia, Canada, or other countries in Europe.

ON TO STANFORD UNIVERSITY AND SILICON VALLEY

Stanford University is in the heart of California's Silicon Valley, the center of America's high-tech industry. Unsure of what subject to pursue there, Brin soon found a passion for internet technologies and search engines. He wrote papers alone and with others about ways to extract information and retrieve large amounts of data. But he took his analysis to the next level when he developed his own software. His experimental work was turning into real work.

Google cofounder Larry Page, shown here, and other technology leaders met with President-Elect Donald Trump in December 2016 in New York City to ensure their companies would not be hurt by the Trump administration's policies.

In 1995, he met Larry Page at a meeting of prospective doctoral students in computer science. They did not like each other at first, even when Brin was assigned to serve as Page's on-campus companion. They argued about everything. Eventually, they discovered that extracting information from large data collections interested them both. They put aside any differences and became friends. In January 1996, they began to collaborate on a research project with the goal of finding a better way to get information on the web. They based their project on the assumption that popular information mattered:

they ranked search term results by page popularity, that is, by the frequency of a word's appearance on the page. They developed a formula and launched a search engine they called BackRub. They made it available to Stanford students, and soon this project was all Page and Brin could think about.

GOOGLE IS BORN

BackRub was not a very memorable name. So Brin and Page asked a friend, Sean Anderson, for a replacement. He offered the name Googolplex, a reference to the mathematical term "googol"—a one followed by a hundred zeroes—to demonstrate the vast amount of information available online. Brin and Page liked the name but shortened it to Googol. When Anderson searched the term to see if it was an available name, he misspelled it as Google. They registered the name Google.com, first linked to Stanford in September 1997.

Page's dorm room became the data center and Brin's the business office. They still saw Google as a tool for their doctoral dissertations, but it was getting very popular among Stanford students. Brin and Page maxed out their credit cards and hovered by the Stanford loading dock, looking to see who had ordered computers in hopes of snagging some for themselves. They were out of resources.

At first, Brin and Page tried to sell Google to other search engines. They approached Altavista, Yahoo, and Excite, three popular search engines at that time, but the companies weren't interested. Fate was taking them in a different direction.

They took matters into their own hands and developed their own business plan for Google. One of their computer science professors introduced them to Andy Bechtolsheim, then a vice president at Cisco Systems (and later a cofounder of Sun Microsystems with Vinod Khosla). Bechtolsheim liked what he saw and gave the

SILICON VALLEY ATTRACTS IMMIGRANT ENTREPRENEURS

Silicon Valley is a melting pot of diverse cultures and a center for the start-up business that has made it famous. This is largely because of the reputation of Stanford University in Palo Alto, said to be the country's top high-tech university. The university attracts immigrant students like Brin to the area. Silicon Valley, many believe, is a state of mind and not just a physical location. It attracted Pramod Sharma, an immigrant from India. Sharma cofounded a start-up named Osmo, which teaches children the basics of computer coding. For Sharma, Silicon Valley's advantage is that it encourages experimentation and the freedom to be creative.[4]

young entrepreneurs a check for $100,000, the first major investment in Google.[3]

In September 1998, Google became an official company, Google Inc. Page became CEO and Brin, president. They rented a garage from Brin's girlfriend's sister, Susan Wojcicki, in Menlo Park, California. It didn't take long before the industry noticed what these Stanford dropouts—much to their parents' dismay—were up to businesswise. *PC Magazine* named Google one of the top one hundred best websites and search engines of 1998.

EXPANSION REQUIRES INVESTMENT

The following year the company already required new office space, and it moved to Palo Alto. Brin and Page knew they needed more money to expand, but they didn't want investors to take control of the company. They found two venture capital firms that could meet their terms: Sequoia Capital and Kleiner Perkins Caufield & Byers. By 2001, other management decisions had to be made. Industry veteran and former Sun Microsystems chief technology officer Eric Schmidt took over as CEO of the company, while Page moved over to head up product development, and Brin took charge as president of technology. Under Schmidt's leadership, Google produced its first profits.

The company went public in 2004 and made both Brin and Page billions of dollars. Google has become the most popular search engine in the world. Brin focuses on the company's innovations like self-driving cars and networks of balloons to bring the internet to less-developed countries. Page and Brin established a parent company for Google called Alphabet. Page is CEO, and Brin is president.

Brin is now considered the richest immigrant in the country, worth nearly $40 billion, and the tenth richest person in America.[5] Like many other entrepreneurs, he is involved with philanthropy. He has donated $1 million to the Hebrew Immigrant Aid Society that helped his family get to the United States. He and his now ex-wife, Anne, established the Brin Wojcicki Foundation with more than $1 billion in assets. They have also donated heavily to the Michael J. Fox Foundation for Parkinson's Research. Both Brin's mother and great-aunt suffered from the disease. Brin is involved in social entrepreneurship to solve problems related to the environment, women's issues, and education. The Brin Wojcicki Foundation also provides resources to end poverty in the San Francisco Bay Area, including Meals on Wheels and the Boy's and Girl's clubs, soup kitchens, and homeless shelters.[6]

CHAPTER NOTES

INTRODUCTION

1. Stuart Anderson, "Forty Percent of Fortune 500 Companies Founded by Immigrants or Their Children," Forbes.com, June 19, 2011, https://www.forbes.com/sites/stuartanderson/2011/06/19/40-percent-of-fortune-500-companies-founded-by-immigrants-or-their-children/#14eaf87b4a59.
2. Ibid.

CHAPTER 1. LEVI STRAUSS MAKES AMERICAN DENIM PANTS FAMOUS

1. Harold Evans, Gail Buckland, and David Lefer, *They Made America* (New York, NY and Boston, MA: Little, Brown & Company, 2004), p. 110.
2. Ibid., 111.
3. Ibid., 111.
4. Ibid., 112.
5. Ibid., 112.
6. Ibid., 113.

CHAPTER 2. ANDREW CARNEGIE BECOMES THE QUINTESSENTIAL CAPTAIN OF INDUSTRY

1. "Andrew Carnegie's Story," Carnegie.org, https://www.carnegie.org/interactives/foundersstory/#!/.
2. Ibid.
3. Ibid.
4. "People and Events: The Homestead Strike," PBS.org, http://www.

pbs.org/wgbh//amex/carnegie/peopleevents/pande04.html.

5. "Andrew Carnegie's Story."

6. "American Experience: Andrew Carnegie, Rags to Riches Timeline," http://www.pbs.org/wgbh//amex/carnegie/timeline/f_timeline. html.

7. "Andrew Carnegie's Story."

8. Ibid.

9. Ibid.

CHAPTER 3. ALEXANDER GRAHAM BELL GETS WIRED

1. Edwin S. Grosvenor and Morgan Wesson, *Alexander Graham Bell: The Life and Times of the Man Who Invented the Telephone* (New York, NY: Harry N. Abrams, 1997), p. 23.

2. Ibid., 67.

3. "Columbia Welcoming the Nations," NYTimes.com, http://www. nytimes.com/learning/general/onthisday/harp/0520.html.

4. Edwin S. Grosvenor and Morgan Wesson, *Alexander Graham Bell*, p. 72-73.

5. "Alexander Graham Bell Biography," Biography.com, http://www. biography.com/people/alexander-graham-bell-9205497.

CHAPTER 4. AN WANG'S INVESTMENT PAYS OFF

1. An Wang with Eugene Linden, *Lessons: An Autobiography* (Reading, MA: Addison Wesley, 1986), p. 12.

2. Ibid., p. 25.

3. Dennis Hevesi, "An Wang, 70, Is Dead of Cancer; Inventor and Maker of Computers," *New York Times*, March 25, 1990, http://www.nytimes.com/1990/03/25/obituaries/an-wang-

70-is-dead-of-cancer-inventor-and-maker-of-computers. html?pagewanted=print.

6. Hevesi, "An Wang."

7. Ibid.

8. Susan Lammers, "Review of Lessons: An Autobiography by Dr. An Wang with Eugene Linden," *Los Angeles Times*, January 18 1987, http://articles.latimes.com/1987-01-18/books/bk-5392_1_wang-laboratories.

9. An Wang with Eugene Linden, *Lessons: An Autobiography*.

10. Hevesi, "An Wang."

CHAPTER 5. ANDY GROVE: FROM REFUGEE TO THRIVING BUSINESSMAN

1. Joshua Cooper Ramo, "Andrew Grove: A Survivor's Tale," *Time*, December 29. 1997, http://content.time.com/time/subscriber/printout/0,8816,987588,00.html.

2. Tim Lister, "Today's Refugees Follow Path of Hungarians Who Fled Soviets in 1956," CNN.com, September 7, 2015, http://www.cnn.com/2015/09/07/europe/hungary-refugees-1956/.

3. Ramo, "Andrew Grove."

4. Ibid.

5. Dean Takahashi, "Silicon Valley Legend and Former Intel CEO Andy Grove Passes Away at 79," VentureBeat.com, March 21, 2016, http://venturebeat.com/2016/03/21/silicon-valley-legend-and-former-intel-ceo-andy-grove-passes-away-at-79/.

6. Andrew S. Grove, *Only the Paranoid Survive* (New York, NY: Currency/Doubleday, 1996), p. vii-x.

7. Mark Rivett-Carnac, "The True Story of Intel Pioneer Andrew Grove, TIME's 1997 Man of the Year," *Time*, March 22, 2016, http://time.com/4267150/andrew-grove-intel-survivor-biography-budapest/.

CHAPTER 6. ARIANNA HUFFINGTON NAVIGATES HER WAY TO MEDIA MOGUL

1. William D. Cohan, "How Arianna Huffington Lost Her Newsroom," *Vanity Fair*, September 7, 2016, http://www.vanityfair.com/news/2016/09/how-arianna-huffington-lost-her-newsroom.
2. "Arianna Huffington Biography," Biography.com, http://www.biography.com/people/arianna-huffington-21216537.
3. Ibid.
4. Ibid.
5. William D. Cohan, "The Inside Story of Why Arianna Huffington Left the Huffington Post," *Vanity Fair*, September 8, 2016, http://www.vanityfair.com/news/2016/09/why-arianna-huffington-left-the-huffington-post.
6. Ibid.
7. Ibid.
8. Ibid.
9. "Despite Challenges Immigrant Women Are Experiencing Amazing Entrepreneurial Success," NWBC.gov, https://www.nwbc.gov/content/despite-challenges-immigrant-women-are-experiencing-amazing-entrepreneurial-success.
10. Luisa Kroll, "American Dreamers: Foreign Born Women Making Fortunes in U.S.," Forbes.com, June 8, 2015, https://www.forbes.com/sites/luisakroll/2015/06/09/american-dreamers-foreign-born-women-making-fortunes-in-u-s/#a9321aea9321.
11. Ibid.
12. "2016 America's Richest Self-Made Women: Neerja Sethi," Forbes.com, https://www.forbes.com/profile/neerja-sethi/?list=self-made-women.
13. "2016 America's Richest Self-Made Women: Diane von Furstenberg," Forbes.com, https://www.forbes.com/profile/diane-von-furstenberg/?list=self-made-women.

"2016 America's Richest Self-Made Women: Peggy Cherng," Forbes.com, https://www.forbes.com/profile/peggy-cherng/?list=self-made-women.

15. "2016 American's Richest Self-Made Women: Sonia Gardner," Forbes.com, https://www.forbes.com/profile/sonia-gardner/?list=self-made-women.

CHAPTER 7. VINOD KHOSLA MENTORS NEW ENTREPRENEURS

1. "Forbes 400: Romesh T. Wadhani," Forbes.com, https://www.forbes.com/profile/romesh-t-wadhwani/.

2. Matthew Herper, "An Opioid Spray Showered Billionaire John Kapoor in Riches. Now He's Feeling the Pain," Forbes.com, October 4, 2016, https://www.forbes.com/sites/matthewherper/2016/10/04/death-kickbacks-and-a-billionaire-the-story-of-a-dangerous-opioid/#2a0941736e3f.

3. "Forbes 400: John Kapoor," Forbes.com, https://www.forbes.com/profile/john-kapoor/.

4. Steven Mufson, "Billionaire Vinod Khosla's Big Dreams for Biofuels Fail to Catch Fire," *Washington Post*, November 28, 2014, https://www.washingtonpost.com/business/economy/billionaire-vinod-khoslas-big-dreams-for-biofuels-fail-to-catch-fire/2014/11/27/04899d12-69d7-11e4-9fb4-a622dae742a2_story.html?utm_term=.0e920c9ae5ac.

5. Ibid.

6. Bill Snyder, "Vinod Khosla: Be Wary of 'Stupid Advice,'" Stanford Graduate School of Business, May 28, 2015, https://www.gsb.stanford.edu/insights/vinod-khosla-be-wary-stupid-advice.

7. "Social Entrepreneurship, Vinod Khosla, Khosla Ventures," Stanford.edu, April 24, 2002, http://ecorner.stanford.edu/videos/29/Social-Entrepreneurship.

8. "Unitus Seed Fund Lands $8 Million for BOP Startups from Leading Early-stage Investors," USF.vc, January 3, 2013, https://usf.vc/updates/january-2013-announcement/.

CHAPTER 8. SERGEY BRIN GOOGLES HIS WAY TO BILLIONAIRE

1. Ari Goldman, "4,000 Soviet Jews Migrated in March, Highest in a Decade," *New York Times*, April 5, 1989, http://www.nytimes.com/1989/04/05/world/4000-soviet-jews-migrated-in-march-highest-in-a-decade.html.
2. "Sergey Brin Biography: Success Story of Google Co-Founder," AstrumPeople.com, https://astrumpeople.com/serbey-brin-biography/.
3. Ibid.
4. Elizabeth Lee, "Silicon Valley Culture Attracts Immigrants," VOANews.com, July 12, 2016, http://www.voanews.com/a/immigrants-drawn-to-silicon-valley-culture/3413931.html.
5. "Forbes 400: Sergey Brin," Forbes.com, https://www.forbes.com/profile/sergey-brin/?list=forbes-400.
6. "Tech Philanthropy Guide: Sergey Brin," InsidePhilanthropy.com, https://www.insidephilanthropy.com/guide-to-individual-donors/sergey-brin.html.

GLOSSARY

algorithm A computation to solve a problem.

alumnus A graduate of a school, college, university, or other educational program.

chairman The person elected to head up a company's board of directors.

chief executive officer (CEO) The person appointed to head up a company.

coke A product made from coal that is vital to the manufacture of steel.

computer-aided design An engineering software application for manufacturing.

dissertations Lengthy research-based documents needed to obtain PhD degrees.

dividends The money a company pays to stockholders from its earnings.

handloom A manually operated means of weaving.

hydrofoil A sleek and light vessel whose hull lifts out of the water.

integrated circuit A system of electronic components on a single chip to perform a particular function.

liberty ships US cargo ships originally used by the Merchant Marines in World War II.

MBA A master's in business administration, an advanced business degree.

microfinance A means of providing funding to start-ups that would ordinarily not qualify for loans.

Moore's law An observation made by Gordon Moore in the mid-1960s about the rate of change in the miniaturization of transistors in integrated circuits.

philanthropy The act of donating money or property to others, usually nonprofit organizations.

Pinkerton An employee of the Pinkerton Detective Agency, usually hired to stop resistance or crime.

quintessential The perfect example of a trait or characteristic.

rivet A device made of metal to securely hold two things together.

router Hardware or software necessary to transfer data between two or more machines.

scarlet fever A contagious, severe disease that causes fever and a red rash, usually affecting children.

semiconductor The base of an integrated circuit

social entrepreneurship The act of financing initiatives, often directed at lifting people from poverty or improving the environment.

start-up A new entrepreneurial business venture, often financed with funding from outside sources.

venture capital Funds made available to help a new company start its operations.

FURTHER READING

BOOKS

Alvarez, Pilar. *New Jobs, New Opportunities: British Immigrants Arrive in America, 1830s-1890s* (Spotlight on Immigration and Migration). New York, NY: Rosen Publishing, 2016.

Balog, Tom. *Indian Immigrants* (Immigration to North America). Broomall, PA: Mason Crest, 2017.

Brezina, Corona. *Sergey Brin, Larry Page, Eric Schmidt, and Google* (Internet Biographies). New York, NY: Rosen Publishing, 2012.

Byers, Ann. *Immigration: Interpreting the Constitution* (Understanding the United States Constitution). New York, NY: Rosen Publishing, 2015.

Faulkner, Nicholas. *101 Entrepreneurs and Business Leaders*. New York, NY: Britannica Educational Publishing, 2016.

Gan, Jiao. *Chinese Immigrants* (Immigration to North America). Broomall, PA: Mason Crest, 2016.

Gifford, Jonathan. *100 Great Business Leaders*. Singapore: Marshall Cavendish, 2013.

Jackson, Aurelia. *Google: How Larry Page & Sergey Brin Changed the Way We Search the Web*. Broomall, PA: Mason Crest, 2015.

Kent, Zachary. *Andrew Carnegie: Industrialist and Philanthropist* (Legendary American Biographies). New York, NY: Enslow Publishers, 2015.

Pierro, Martin T. and Nick Justis. *Arianna Huffington*. Vancouver, WA: Bluewater Comics, 2011.

Wolff, Ariana. *Khan Academy and Salman Khan* (Internet Biographies). New York, NY: Rosen Publishing, 2015.

WEBSITES

The Carnegie Corporation of New York

Carnegie.org

The Carnegie Corporation of New York started in 1911 to promote international peace and growth of knowledge, two of Scottish immigrant Andrew Carnegie's major concerns. Learn how Carnegie's legacy continues through various funds and foundations.

Forbes Magazine

forbes.com/sites/luisakroll/2015/06/09/american-dreamers-foreign-born-women-making-fortunes-in-u-s/#a9321aea9321

In this feature article from business publication *Forbes*, learn how women born outside the United States contribute to the American economy while making their own American dreams for success come true. Of particular note are the obstacles immigrant women must overcome.

Harvard Business Review

hbr.org/2016/10/why-are-immigrants-more-entrepreneurial

A recent research study featured in the *Harvard Business Review* explores why immigrants are twice as likely as US-born citizens to launch new businesses. Learn why cross-cultural experience makes a difference.

Levi Strauss and Co.

levistrauss.com

From the invention of the blue jean in 1873 to a current focus on sustainability, Levi Strauss and Co. honors its heritage to reinvent sturdy clothing for new generations. Learn the history of the company and what it stands for in the twenty-first century.

Voice of America

voanews.com/a/immigrants-drawn-to-silicon-valley-culture/3413931. html

This feature article from international broadcaster Voice of America discusses the importance of immigrants to California's Silicon Valley area. Learn how immigrants bring innovation and a sense of play to new products.

INDEX

ABOUT THE AUTHOR

BARBARA KRASNER

Barbara Krasner holds an MFA in writing for children and young adults from the Vermont College of Fine Arts. She is the author of more than twenty books for young readers. She teaches immigration literature and history in New Jersey.